Wintering Over

poems by

Susannah Lee

Finishing Line Press
Georgetown, Kentucky

Wintering Over

ACKNOWLEDGMENTS

Grateful acknowledgment to the editors of the following journals in which some of these poems first appeared:

Cloudbank: "Water Elegy"
Nine Mile Magazine: "The Field," "White Mountains"
North American Review, Open Space, "Night Swim, Tempelfjorden, Svalbard"
The Woven Tale Press: "Votive Notes of Tannin and Blue," "My Secret Herbarium," "Ordo Virtutum"

Publisher: Leah Huete de Maines
Editor: Christen Kincaid
Cover Art: Tom Young
Author Photo: Tom Young
Cover Design: Elizabeth Maines McCleavy

Order online: www.finishinglinepress.com
also available on amazon.com

Author inquiries and mail orders:
Finishing Line Press
PO Box 1626
Georgetown, Kentucky 40324
USA

Contents

I. North

Notes of Tannin and Blue ~ 1

My Secret Herbarium ~ 2

Ordo Virtutum ~ 3

Matins ~ 4

Just as the Light Returns ~ 5

Vigil in Midnight Sun ~ 6

Fjord ~ 7

Night Swim, Tempelfjorden, Svalbard ~ 8

Wild Cloudberry ~ 9

At the Glacier's Edge ~ 10

II. The Field

Days of the Anchoress ~ 13

Aurora ~ 15

White Mountains ~ 16

Second Cut ~ 17

Backyard Rooster ~ 18

Young Bird Mavis ~ 19

The Pack ~ 20

February March ~ 21

Water Elegy ~ 24

The Field ~ 25

AUTHOR'S NOTE

Several years ago, my interest in monastic life and contemplative prayer led me to a story of Carmelite sisters (nine nuns, two novices, and one postulant to be exact) who were relocated from Iceland to northern Norway, high above the Arctic Circle. They arrived with no money and few possessions, but with considerable ingenuity, prayer and devotion to set about funding and building a monastery that was finally consecrated in 1998. Similar resilience and resourcefulness have been witnessed since medieval times among contemplatives like Hildegard von Bingen or Julian of Norwich, but I was somewhat surprised to find that this was a contemporary story.

This narrative sparked my imagining of cloistered lives lived in a fierce climate, with extreme periods of darkness and solitude. As the intention of monastic life has remained relatively unchanged over centuries, I felt a license to time-travel, delving not into the theological so much as the visceral dailiness of lives in the midst of descending darkness, bitter cold, and solitude warmed by devotion and community. Most of the poems of Section One were loosely inspired by the story of these intrepid women.

I. North

What is a prayer but a song of longing
turning on the thread of its own history?

from *Sparrow, My Sparrow* by Jane Mead

NOTES OF TANNIN AND BLUE

We crossed from Iceland to the Arctic circle
despite warnings of inclemency,
each night unveiling at sundown as we were schooled,
& slid into the chink of dusk & melancholy.

It has been my habit to embrace what I fear—
loneliness, darkness, cold, especially cold,
and wind them into my devotions. Oh
yes! distraction plagues me too, which is why

I have assumed the role of scribe,
for when we grow older than memory.
Now and again my illuminations dry
with one stray hair pressed in the oil & cadmium...

In winter, we bow to the Nordic darkness
of smelt and herring bone spines on the icy sea
slapping the barque's sure underbelly.
Last year, I was impervious to extinction.

But come this spring, if you can call it spring,
as if suctioned from peat centuries
before I am meant to be found, hands folded
at my shallow chest in supplication—

I am, as it turns out, a good supplicant
always asking, asking again and again—
I will be returned to my bed of muskeg
still tawny like the owl that visits my dreams.

After evensong I am nearly stone deaf with song and seal my lips
with unguents to gentle my body for preservation and sleep.
On that first night I heard thunder that would fracture
my skull from its very veins, and later my heart.

In the dark this night I turn to my sisters,
and summon the litanies of ice and smoke welling within us.

MY SECRET HERBARIUM

Do you know that under my bed I preserve the flora
I have come to love, pressed between sheer paper flimsies
I sneak from the scriptorium? Some I snug under heavy
parchment, festered then thinned by a flowing bath.

Such a curious process to sour the cloth into oblivion
then raise it again! I have seen its flaxen shade
in the sails that wave turning into the wind.
How small they become is up to them.

Or, from time to time we curry the found skins
of arctic fox or deer who have leapt their last. These we treasure
with blessings for they hold spin & stealth in every fiber.
So much that my pen and brush cavort & sway as music

reduces me to my tears. In prayer I ask water
to run swiftly, run pure for this will bind our world
as it softens the vellum. See how circular is my thinking!
Sometimes I cannot get beyond it and pray for release…

At night I number the gifts that God has given me,
dream them here for time immemorial. Saxifrage,
Caribou moss—I ride high on the withers and remember
this view for my Book of Hours, steep as the fjords

who are my cousins, lash down to the sea with a daring
I deeply love. In this shelter of time I tend my herbarium
praising each bloom for its courage. As such I am schooled
by the lichen to seek light in the most meager of places…

the brief loft of heat and the darkest indelible.

ORDO VIRTUTUM

In a warm spring such as this, cotton grass in ecstasy stows light
        away for midwinter. As do I. You might wonder how I do this?

I cannot easily divulge to you, nor myself,
        I just know it to be so. Like the cinnamon grape

that buoys our communion wine, skins fermented
        then ground to pigment, shimmer a twilight green.

Today I crossed the wooly caterpillar, freed from ice
        on her seven years to moth-hood! Mesmerizing

and familiar. Her wings will be so plain. My wings too are plain
        and my weight in the world so utterly mine.

Which leads me to the fulcrum of prayer. Come morning,
        when the wingspan of mystics lifts us

in the choir stall and we deliver the *Ordo Virtutum*
        I will resonate this plainchant for you, arms outstretched.

Our shelter here at last in consecration stands
        awaiting the trance that must and will consume our walls,

corridors, ante chambers, even the old buttery—
        the obsidian milk glass topples from its shelf,

shatters while we sing sorrow back
        underground, beneath the glacier of dawn.

MATINS

I woke with a start—darkness enveloped the sanctuary,
        my dream rushed down to the inlet shore.

Slippered, I follow—what had woken me whispered
        in a thrown voice. A ventriloquism I longed for,

the speaking of icons at water's edge
        as the bear dips a paw in the icy flow. I saw the gill net pull

with the force of sound binding my heart. This was not a dream.
        Rising from the frazil ice, those exquisite shards of cold,

was the crystalline song of bones lifted by the thousands.
        Schooling fish. An opera of motion that roiled my Soul.

Matins came, but I stayed with the bones.
        Bones to our bones so that we could swim upright.

So that we might pray to the opposite shore and hear
        the repeat of Ages down from us—

sounding the mineral and liquid night of what is to come.

JUST AS THE LIGHT RETURNS

Springtime our song heats up pink the moss campion,
permafrost swallows our toes. How good this feels
when we rush to Compline at the end of day—
nearly as luscious as the psalmody breath itself.

Knitting the scent of sphagnum and sand laced with fog, I ask
Am I cold? Am I warm? I wonder this often. But they tell me
not to query myself so much. Spring, you see, presents
a whole host of new miracles—the senses divide, dissolve,

sail out on their own bright skiffs. I see stars mingling in the sky.
We have journeyed from darkness to darkness, I remind the others
by echoing the silence of my prayer.

Yet now my bearings are so medievally atilt
I coddle the eggs with juniper,
jump when the spigot spews rust, imagining
my dear mother in her day dress just that shade.

My palate too is askew, mystifying
memory of seaweed pudding I will steam for dinner tonight.
A pinch of nutmeg just explodes the sea whip kelp
we gather on the beaches. By dinner time I am a wreck

of excitement, pray for calm to set my path and the pudding.
Not much of a cook they whisper, but wait,
I will show them that they can taste, actually taste
darkness that has tempered this thin firmament.

VIGIL IN MIDNIGHT SUN

2 am. In the kitchen garden spatulas of chard herald
        the pure bewilderment in my heart today.

Rising to light we had bathed in all night I bowed my head
        to the letter S curling around me like a tendril

of pea snap. Illuminated as Sorrow and Swept I understood
        why keeping house uplifted my spirit so—

I, reluctant apostle of gold, opened shutters to air,
        and light stunned blind the chamber so that I might see.

Everywhere the weight of objects took my breath.
        Silent. Corporeal. You could taste it.

But I am called to work on prayer and umbra,
        put my palette down, then wept great satchels of despair.

By now you realize I am a novice. In broad daylight
        I attend and bless the utter darkness rising

just below the purpling horizon—O sullen narwhal
        who cannot ever break the surface before its gilded tusk.

FJORD

Formed by abrasion. Upheavals often.

Waters flowing east on the surface, west just below.
    This knowledge, this counterpoint of sea

is precisely where a smidgen of girl named A, as in *always*, slipped
    from the dory that ferried her out. An old oarlock

and wind chimes intoning the air. Severance is divine
    she told me. Battens and a tarpaulin were her mantle, a sail.

She was not afraid. Not of the cautionary, nor the rubric flapping
    recklessly out her window. Always she tied the sash back at night

in her mother's house where nesting wax wings toppled
    mercilessly from the lintel each spring. Always a little bedraggled,

she inclined with the attitude of tailwind, frothy not obdurate
    and heading due north where her ancestors waited,

dimpling flaxen quilts with waxed thread and quick elbow knots.
    Mother, she said, mother was pure owl descending blind and sure

as scree. We hugged the shoreline in a tempest once, I a limpet
    hoarding the sheer rock face with little faith in the watery strait,

she homing along the gunwale for the sure stroke to bring us about.
    I sang to the cauled wake behind us, cradling the weight of

afterlife in my arms.

NIGHT SWIM, TEMPELFJORDEN, SVALBARD

Something preceded me as I plunged
into meltwater so smooth, beyond glacial. I saw

light where there was none. I cut
into darkness to descend faster than heart

beat. My body signaled silence. When I came up
to air I saw the fjord shift imperceptibly—

the fox grey earth barely holding all
it had seen. Ancient spirits flew up

toppled, spun with kittiwake and guillemot
shelving off from the glacier's eyes

down to the tumbled scree of my heart.
And they buoyed me. Here, I am not allowed to die.

WILD CLOUDBERRY

opens in air to a blue pulse of sea surrounding
us here. Iron Age veins still warm through schist

and spongy mire I harvest cloudberry, sing down
to my shoes as I walk the salt-laced earth.

Here I have a frost garden, circular
in arcs of tender lichen and moss. I lift my skirts,

tie the bulk and air of them at my hip with a nesting
of cloudberry I will simmer into nighttime.

Here I am brimful, holding no secrets between
all things for which I sing. One day I'll be found

dreaming deep beneath layers of licheny peat
with the amber cloudberry forever puzzling that smile

mother called beatitude and told me was my resting face.
But I did not rest when I was young. This patinaed world,

this tumbled doing and undoing of tides
always rang truer. I'll go on living for this,

the brief interval, the cradling sorrow leaves behind,
and for the crescent sea dive of desire. For unsafety,

disappearance. I am willed into song.
And for the fruit that opens thereafter.

AT THE GLACIER'S EDGE

Today I am mute but operatic, take a turn and rise to the dark,
which is a future I have stopped probing for the time being,

being so clouded and blood-raw at once, like the great bear
brushing past sleep with redolent musk, nearly floral but not.

I pivot toward its magnitude until it stares back
over its shoulder with the white face of death.

Death of the loved one, of the great bear, of the mother silent
in childbirth. Tell me once again please about hibernal glory

so that we might rest, then venture on in darkness and cold.
Tell me about pilgrimage with unopened tins of rockfish,

and love enough to go around. Listen for ice melt thunder
with courage to hold in the palms of our hands.

Night has rolled down on night, on eventide, on day,
so I will gather pearl ash and leaven for the flock of us in flight,

keep an eye on the hunter who cinches this incomparable dark
like a tourniquet. Have we forgotten terror

here in this deepest solitude? Have we forgotten the ice-pilling
wool of cloak, waistband, and failure? Let us never forget

the look of the bear as it drowns beneath the weight
of our dreams. This might be the incipit emerging

to sound once again. Or all our endings lined up
like hungry schoolchildren with empty knapsacks of hope.

So it begins.

II. The Field

DAY OF THE ANCHORESS

I

Today the scent of jonquils conjures a table here in the corner
so that I might invite you in...

To be truthful, weeks maybe months go by when no one visits
and I become lost in song. Do you hear the melody threading

its way when you walk by? Each leek and greening fruit in your basket
washed with the loving cloth of my gentle air. Some days, I imagine

I race you home just for the chance to step over your threshold first,
let you in, *I can take it from here*, I say,

knowing that you are grateful to relinquish the weight of your day.

II

Today the mirror of my soul is too much with me.
As I roll my eyes in dimness, a threnody emerges

risen from this very dirt, an element charged
with cesium-bright sorrow so exquisite I feel my muscles contract

as if to prepare for the crowning of a newborn. Blood flows.
My sacrum aches. Times like these I send visitors away.

Even the old stray cat looks up
from chewing unseen fleas and runs for the hills.

III

Today? I don't know today, my mother whispered
as she lay dying, damp with concentration.

(In here the weight of time is gone, no oxygen to make it burn.)

IV

Today I don't know today, its rough contour
like the grainy quince you'll simmer into jam.

Only the body keeps its awkward will and bone— the pull of solitude
on flesh as I watch it skew recklessly up my legs and arms,

taking measure of me, stone by stone, ounce by finicky ounce.

V

Other days, even angels become disoriented. Like the gaudy ones
in frescoes who ferry the Soul to heaven. Their clunky wings

and oversized limbs might not be up to the task.
As they speed her up through the cumuli, I think

Oh no, she is too light to bear! Then they let go mid-air.
Dear Soul has settled right here, inside my porous solitude.

I think to myself, *Let me clear a place and set it anew.*
When it's time to go, I'll wrap our faithfully salvaged air

and leave it by the threshold. You understand
I always longed for but did not need more.

AURORA

In the beginning there wasn't even an ounce
      of light, not a filament nor whisper of this, just night

fallen heavy and dark—
      I had a child once, and named her Aurora

She clung to my womb as I
      clung to the ship's rail on the Sea of Galilee

Will anyone ever calm this sea?
      Stilled by sleep only while waves pull endlessly,

unaware of the milky song
      I offer for her breath-taking, solemn

vigil of holding what was given,
      as her silent inbreath spread skyward

in fragile river and rung
      reaching my soul, for once and all

the heart stilled within her sanctuary,
      mine now that valley of lyre and wind,

our song marking her sky—
      Aurora of the sky's golden mane, little mare

that gallops mythic and trusting
      in a gale as it lifts each breath, each

willful lightness higher still, and still mine.

WHITE MOUNTAINS
in Memoriam

Open like a prayer-washed canticle

sounding a fricative love for the world
this is the day that the Lord hath made!

She packed her rucksack and set out
not tentative exactly, but not confident

where she was going. She packed a pb & j
and Stanley thermos full. This was the scope of things

and it had the feel of old vellum, the notes
lovingly holding the skin of the journey

with intention, but leaving a lot out as well.
Did she know the end of the trail

would be a compass, would ferry her back
to a beginning? The song unwound

silently at first, then polyphonic
like the wind lifting each light follicle

and the fine gauzy shirt of bravery,
her singular smile

greeted the wind, was carried up
and out to the light but only when earthly

time, its broad history, permitted.

SECOND CUT

The hay is tall enough to conceal
all manner of desire
and sorrow, the runted fawn,
this brief cover settling
on the heart like swaddle. Hold tight,

then let the creatures out
to the parched ragged line of flood tide,
the full swinging breast of mother
approaching her final drop

before nurture turns in the noon day sun.

The goat leaning on rough bark hopes
for salvation from all that binds her,
leaves her gnarly fiber there

then looks to you with something
that might be contempt
but isn't, is rather, monotony
beloved monotony swelling

in the cast of her shadow. Evening,

the melody of dew settling
and the far-off guttural hum
that means, come morning,
the blade will strip us bare.

BACKYARD ROOSTER

If we could just start this day off right,
step out with the rooster, meticulous
in presentation, the ladies tethered
by cochlear tremor spiraling
down through the history of manners...

If we could strut this way and then burst forth
with our cocked basket of cuttings, say,
delphiniums! a delirious blue of blue,
before striking out to deliberate.

Could there be quiet throughout the land, please?
Could the eddy still its pull, the prophet
hold her tongue, the fishmonger
stun the scup with the knife just below the eye?
Let the feasting table be set!

This is a moment, framed and hungry.
Guests may arrive or not, it hardly matters,
but when the bright feathers settle
in their weightlessness, and the thief

runs off silently content, we in wonder turn
to discover we are utterly starving, and alone.

YOUNG BIRD MAVIS

Sometimes when she thinks too much, the pinions open and spin,
spread out to the bright sky with weightlessness and ardor. Then
she prays that the bird of her bones comes down to earth in time
for dinner when the bread has risen and soup is warm.

Now and again, there's the problem of the moult which happens
with little warning. But she's learned she can walk away instead.
Solitude lures her from the playground, the jungle gym strung
with luminous bodies making her dizzy and blind—

As petticoat and skirt unfurl, she loses her bearings and fear.
In the old roost, dust motes illuminate summer air like citrines,
celestial and animated by her love of being there alone.
When the voice calls her home, a bewildering yodel designed

to ransom every lost soul within earshot, she won't answer, not now.
She has learned this from the inside out. Brought earthward
for the final tally, all parts of her still intact spin hungry
and courageous folding up, braced for the fall.

THE PACK

Unleashed from capture they ran the field
with Muybridge momentum
                              hunger quadrillioned
in the neurons that brought them forth.
                              How they sped
past the horse with one hoof bent idle,
barely turned heads to catch the
                                        redolence of pig.
The solipsism of mud and splendor of baptism
at a nearby pond might have slowed them but no,
                                        they onward.
Carry them on their cast of line angling out,

tongues spittle-lipped and so determined that their own
whelping rises up in every breath.
                              Anoint them
as they gather burr and tick,
a tendon ripped on wire so barbed this alone
                              would mock
our singular intention to cultivate this
land, call it home.

FEBRUARY MARCH
near Old Deerfield, Massachusetts

I

Cardinal of one
wallow me down to the river

with your sweet tone.
The wintry winds howl

but you rest autumnal in the quince.
How so little resists this velocity!

Round about this time even the hunger moon
is brittle with apology.

Round about this time I think forced march,
souls with little else but skinned

deer on their feet. Girls barely grown
scraping off fear enough

to hurl themselves into darkness.
What water ran beneath their feet

didn't sting them to the core
before slaking thirst?

II

All tracks covered over,
the drift becomes both way in

and way out, becomes
chimera and forgetfulness.

In this darkest cold
when the wind steals breath,

erases our way on,
the breaking snow whispers

Shhh! Shhh! Shhh!
the moonless moon has turned

to embrace the dark. This is a gift.
We must carry on.

III

Traveling north,
deeper notes from the glacier

sound, a lost goat settles in the snow
and grows quiet,

the moose calf delirious
and hungry, loses its way.

If the origin of theft is sleuth—
silver fox, bear and fisher cat

the slivered moon gone dark—
these increments

deliver us to countries we have
never seen before.

IV

It was not meant
to be this way.

We were never meant
to be redeemed

without our brothers
and sisters,

the naked secrets
of the forest,

the deep and abiding
cold within our hearts

still singing on.

WATER ELEGY
After Ryuichi Sakamoto

North was the signature we inherited,
          not a blessing but a kinship with lamps

illuminating the hollow wick of nightfall. The febrile
          night rising like steam from a croup kettle

seeking to heal. We sanctioned the dark
          with fever, visions of light, wheat fields

with bobolinks nesting late into the harvest,
          a peony dropping its great globe of flower all at once.

Heat became us. We understood this and chose
          to hoard it with prayers of mercy,

as if earth could hold a very warm mantle of snow,
          as if the prayer wheel spun without touch or wind.

Compass point that defines all others. North,
          when the river flood carries the yew and its roots

downstream whole and expectant, and the rain soaked
          willow releases from the weight of abundance,

keels and rises with the dark earth of its own loss.
          When the seas come to meet us, what sacred text

will we safeguard? What echo in what clear vein
          will we ping our pulsing song back to life?

THE FIELD

So small this expanse of open view, funny
she thought that had something to do with enlightenment

but no, it held the barter system in its gleaming
bone-washed teeth, ripping flesh from truth.

Adjudication, I told her and she wept for the stern
cellular division, bilateral stand-off

she would never want to call home. But the fact was,
it was. A field of view so parsed each creature

was annotated in its arrival and departure
from the water source. They drink daily and go home,

some are killed on the road. And the bone washer
sleeps in a kind of incessant reverie so distant

from the field, he inhabits only his canine flash
and tear, dropping down farther into sleep

forelegs whisking as though escape was the only purpose
to the horizon. The spine hollowed to a whistle,

air is speaking down that long corridor of ritual
that brings it both farther away and close at the same time.

Bone washer, name sayer,
what I wish for you are the wings that will both

carry and reverberate with the tremors
that bring us on.

*   *   *

In the slurry that flushed past the window the night
of the flood, who knows how many misfirings and amputations

had bled into the stream that curdled past the well. This was age-old,
we drank from the well. The fly-catcher knew it.

And the small wingéd fledglings that emptied out into dusk
dipped past the source. This tangy repertoire so helplessly

New World, I too stretched my own forked flight
and said prayers just as my grandmother had and hers

before her, heralding death each evening
with the well-oiled grace of someone stirring up gratitude,

as though it and only it would save you.

* * *

It was the glacial formations and how they had been used
centuries later that moved them. The stone runs

were clearly made for domesticated animals, surging in
with hunger or fear or simply a return to where

they could go no farther. The dark woods abounded with sounds
of ash against ash, old bough sounds

that mimicked the call of a black bear yearling
cast from its den. He would travel, travel

down to the field unsure of what he needed,
forage or flesh, and snag a goat, Capra Domesticus

(sweet and heavy in her tender unawares)

but being so uncertain would retract claws and retreat
leaving the goat to die in the field.

In as much as I understood
the bear's quandary as he ran away mistaken

I blessed his sole dark run out
through hunger, I blessed the goat as she turned

her flat goat neck up to the sky and saw the end
itself a mark of arrival.

* * *

Back when the road first came through
it likely brought with it sows, does and all manner

of prognosticators down the hill, wheeling slowly
because ruts were inevitable, and if not filled

with rainwater gushing and undermining the whole effort,
then hell on the whole machine.

Now the macadam is pressed annually every summer
with oil and puddingstone and left to stink

until use wears it down into itself. Cars hitting the level
where it joins the field spring up with a kind of reckless joy.

As I tell you this a great blue heron carries the air
on its primordial span across the divide

and folds up like origami in the weeping cherry.
Seriously, this could kill you with wonder

and the macular prayer that sits with me
surrenders a lot to memory and then walks on.

* * *

After searing drought and drenching rains,
the old oak and maple give up what buoys them most,

letting go where sessile limbs have gradually opened
too much and often to the elements. She cried out

at the leafy crash that could be a cub descending
but nothing so gamey and pulsing here.

Smack dab on the tarmac from fifty feet
blows the spongy branch to bits. This a map, I tell her,

smitten with age, the reliquary of our love,
one to another.

NOTES

Ordo Virtutum

Ordo Virtutum ("*Order of Virtues*") a sacred music allegory composed (c1151) by the medieval abbess and mystic Hildegard Von Bingen for the consecration of her Abbey in Rupertsberg, Germany.

Night Swim, Tempelfjorden, Svalbard

Templelfjorden is a fjord in the Svalbard archipelago, approximately half way between northern Norway and the North Pole. Due to the fragile permafrost that covers most of Svalbard, bodies will not decompose, and regulations require that the deceased be flown back to the mainland for burial or cremation. A poorly reported newspaper story gave rise to the myth that one could not die on Svalbard.

February March

This poem holds at its heart to the pre-dawn raid in 1704, by French soldiers and Native allies upon the settlement of Deerfield, Massachusetts, also the Pocumtuck homeland. 112 men, women and children were seized as captives and marched 300 miles through the grueling winter to Montreal. Many captives died or were killed along the way, and of those who survived, some were later redeemed and returned home to Deerfield. Nearly one third, chose to stay and live among their captors.

Water Elegy

In 2017, Japanese composer Ryuichi Sakamoto released his 19th studio album "async " following recovery from throat cancer. The piano featured on this album had been rescued from a flooded school gymnasium in Miyagi Prefecture following the devastating earthquake and subsequent Tsunami of 2011. Known as the Tsunami Piano, the instrument had been ravaged by floodwaters that devasted much of Japan's eastern seaboard. Sakamoto died March 28th, 2023.

WITH THANKS

In October of 2022, I was invited by The Arctic Circle to join a late fall sailing expedition to the Svalbard Archipelago along with 29 other artists, writers, and science educators. There I experienced the mythic landscape and pressing realities of the high Arctic, and my life was forever changed. My deepest gratitude to Aaron O'Connor of The Arctic Circle for his support, making this journey possible. Thanks also to my fellow shipmates aboard the barquentine Antigua: the masterful guides and crew; and the participants who entertained, inspired, and at times collaborated or respectfully held space for one another's vision.

To Sister Hedvig and the sisters of Karmel Kloster Tromsø, who welcomed me to celebrate their gifts of Spirit with divine prayer, song and conversation. I offer heartfelt thanks.

Closer to home, thanks to all those who have buoyed me on this journey—Jody Stewart for her patience, humor, and keen editorial eye. To Ellen Wilbur, Mary Ellen Kelly, Mary Koncel, Anne McCabe and Mary Fister—much gratitude for all your encouragement. Thank you to Christen Kincaid of Finishing Line Press. And to Tom Young, photographer extraordinaire, and our daughters, Sarah and Rosalee.

Susannah Lee has worked as a writer, editor, and independent producer for radio and film. She was a Fulbright Scholar to Portugal in Screenwriting. Her radio features have aired on the Christian Science Monitor Radio, NPR, WFCR, and Living on Earth. Her poems have appeared in *Ploughshares, Seneca Review, Sonora Review, Nine Mile Magazine, The Woven Tale* and others. In 2022, she was invited to join The Arctic Circle residency to sail the Svalbard Archipelago in the High Arctic North. She currently lives in rural western Massachusetts.

www.ingramcontent.com/pod-product-compliance
Lightning Source LLC
Chambersburg PA
CBHW022049080426
42734CB00009B/1283